The Resilience Journal

A 2-Minute Commitment to Lift Your Entire Day

Amit Sood MD MS FACP

Happier Stronger Kinder

ISBN 13: 978-0-9995525-2-0
ISBN 10: 0-9995525-2-X
Library of Congress Control Number: 2019900011
LCCN Imprint Name: Global Center for Resiliency and Wellbeing,
Rochester, MN

Disclaimer

The information in this book is not intended to substitute a health care
provider's advice or medical care. Please consult your physician or
other health care provider if you are experiencing any symptoms or
have questions pertaining to the information contained in this book.

From the Desk of Dr. Sood

Dear Friend,

I am delighted to share this journal with you to help your journey into resilience. In the first few pages, I intend to provide you a background on resilience and introduce you to some of the core resilience skills.

My two preferred definitions of resilience are:

◊ *Resilience is the core strength you use to lift the load of life*
◊ *Resilience is doing well when you shouldn't be doing well*

Resilience skills upgrade and strengthen your neuronal networks by leveraging your brain's ability to change itself with experience. Just as you can learn math, music, and language, you can learn resilience. I have personally witnessed phenomenal transformation happening among people who have chosen to embrace resilience and the skills that support resilience, including mindfulness, positive psychology, and learning about the neuroscience. Indeed several hundred research studies cumulatively show that enhancing resilience lifts every aspect of your life—physical, emotional, social, occupational, and spiritual.

Globally, researchers and therapists have developed several different resilience programs. Each program has a unique focus and therapeutic process. Common among many programs is an approach to improve attention, bring greater gratitude, compassion, and acceptance, align one's life with a stronger sense of meaning, and cultivate courage. The Resilience Journal I offer has all of these elements, and is based in the Stress Management and Resilience Training (SMART) program developed by me and my team.

SMART is a structured and evidence-based curriculum to enhance self-awareness, focus, and a positive mindset by integrating cutting-edge advances in neurosciences with timeless principles. SMART has been tested and found effective in over two dozen clinical studies to decrease symptoms of stress and anxiety and increase well-being, resilience, mindfulness, happiness, and positive health behaviors. SMART has helped hundreds of thousands of people over the last ten years. The following link summarizes some of the SMART studies:

SMART helps participants with three closely integrated and inter-related steps:

1. Awareness—SMART helps participants learn the neuroscience of stress, particularly as it pertains to understanding some of the maladaptive instincts of our brain. Participants learn three key neural vulnerabilities that create and then multiply our stress and angst. They are: deficits in focus, predisposition to fatigue, and preoccupation with fear. These three predispositions are shared in an uplifting, fun, and easy to understand format, helping participants learn from a neuroscience perspective, the struggles faced by people living in the twenty-first century.

2. Attention—The two organs in the body that need training and workout to remain strong are the heart and the brain. For the heart, the workout is physical activity. For the brain, the workout is training its attention. SMART helps participants develop deeper, focused, undistracted, and intentional attention. Each attention practice is short and is designed to integrate in a person's life. Further, the attention skills are also geared to enhance uplifting emotions. This combination of attention and emotion jogs the entire prefrontal cortex, providing pragmatic skills that are short yet powerful and sticky.

3. Attitude (resilient mindset)—Thinking is the reward for all the hard work of our ancestors in helping us survive and evolve a highly complex brain. Unfortunately, most of our unmentored thoughts flow from one topic to another, in a random and sometimes chaotic state of wandering attention. SMART offers a structured yet flexible construct to anchor your thoughts with the five timeless principles of gratitude, compassion, acceptance, meaning, and forgiveness. Thoughts so anchored help you savor life with gratitude, heal the world and the self with compassion, creatively engage with 'what is,' find and pursue your north star, and free your mind by forgiving others. The emotional intelligence that emerges, fosters deeper relationships, clearer focus, greater energy, better physical health, and enhanced ability to transcend adversity.

The entire SMART theme converges to five specific practices that I will summarize next.

I hope you join me in bringing greater resilience to your life, and through that pursuit, traverse a more fulfilling and meaning-filled journey.

If you wish, you can learn more about SMART at the following websites: resilientoption.com and resiliencetrainer.com.

Take care.

Amit

The Five SMART Skills

The entire SMART theme converges to five core skills. I will first share the skills and then offer a suggested sequence for you to integrate them in your life. The specific practice is italicized and bold. Once fully adapted, all the practices together take only a few minutes of your time during the day.

#1. Morning Gratitude: The moment we wake up, we often get into our gadgets, start acting on our to do list, or begin mind wandering, thinking about the burdensome day ahead. We give back control of our attention to the world. Our morning routine if often associated with rise in adrenaline, with its attendant adverse health consequences. SMART invites you to spend the first two minutes after you wake up thinking about a few people (typically five) in your life, attending to a particular detail about them that you can remember fondly, and sending them your silent gratitude.

Here is a common morning sequence I suggest, before you place your feet on the carpet:
- ◊ **Start deep slow smooth breathing and close your eyes.**
- ◊ **Think about the first person in your life who matters a lot to you. Recall this person's face. Then send this person a silent gratitude for being in your life.**
- ◊ **Second person—get back to the first memory of this person, the first time you saw him or her. Then send your silent gratitude.**
- ◊ **Third person—look into the eyes of this person and notice the color of the eyes. Then send your silent gratitude.**
- ◊ **Think of someone who has passed away who you loved. Give that person a virtual hug. And then send silent gratitude to that person.**
- ◊ **When you are ready, you may open your eyes.**

Each of these aspects is flexible and customizable. For example, if you do not have a pet, you can replace watching the pet with visualizing a happy moment when you were a child as suggested below:

◊ Go back in time and look at a happy moment in your childhood. Recall your hairstyle at that time! And then send a warm hello to your little self.

With practice you are welcome to include work colleagues, even people who may have annoyed you in the past, in your gratitude practice. I believe one of the best ways to prepare for a meeting is to remind yourself why you are grateful to the person you are going to meet. Every time I practice this, my meeting goes much better.

I highly recommend for people to customize this practice after the initial learning, so it becomes their own. Further, morning gratitude can be practiced later during the day and on a busy day you can practice with fewer than five people. The goal is to wake up with intentional attention, and grateful instead of grumpy.

#2. The Two-Minute Rule: The Two-Minute rule is giving two minutes of undivided attention to someone in your life, who deserves that attention but presently isn't getting it. Research shows when we get back from work, we spend less than 90 seconds with our loved ones, before getting busy with the daily chores. Further, we are very likely to try and 'improve them' in this time. All of this pushes them away from us. We are also mind wandering most of the evening, often thinking about work. Thus, we work eight to ten hours a day, and think about work for an additional two to three hours. This isn't what we bargained for, and happens partly because of the way our brain is designed (very active default mode of the brain).

The two-minute rule invites you to break this sequence. Here is how you can do it:

Imagine if you have been away for a month. When you meet your family after that gap, will you be more interested in them? Will you be kinder? Likely, yes isn't it?

With that background, here is the simple two-minute rule practice— Meet your family for the first two minutes as if you haven't seen them for a month.

I do the following to operationalize it:

◊ In the garage, I check my emails, so that is out of the way.

◊ I then remind myself that I am going to meet some very special people I haven't seen for a month.

◊ I try to bring my best self as I enter the home and within the first 30 seconds of being inside, I try to look at the color of the eyes (for two seconds) of my loved ones (this practice makes sure I come physically close to them instead of a distant hello).

◊ In the first two minutes I try to remind them they were in my thoughts when I was away. Sometimes reminding them how they were right also works very well!

◊ Sprinkling appropriate humor or a good story also helps.

The key is to do your best to show you are in a good mood, in a predictable fashion.

I suggest you adapt the above ideas to your personal life. For example, if you live alone, then you can practice this with your pet, a close friend, perhaps even a good neighbor or a colleague. The idea is to meet at least one person during the day with authentic non-judgmental presence. Such presence is very healing and uplifting for both—you and the person receiving your authentic attention. .

Like morning gratitude, the two-minute rule can be practiced at work. For example, you can choose to start the meetings by first connecting with the participants at a personal level. You can also choose to remind others how you were thinking about their idea or how their previous insight helped you. The idea is to convert transactional connections into affiliative ones.

We have three kinds of connections: adversarial, transactional, and affiliative. Adversarial is obvious. Transactional is mostly a business like connection, even at home. Both of these connections do not nurture our minds. The two-minute rule is designed to minimize adversarial connections and convert your transactional connections into affiliative ones, which will not only lift your emotions, but also may enhance your creativity and productivity at work.

#3. Curious Moments: Curiosity is the love of learning. We are here today because our little ones are curious. But as we grow older, our curiosity fades. We start experiencing the world with our ingrained biases. That is when we stop learning and growing. Curious moments is a way to overcome the fragmentation in attention that happens these days to us with screen overload. Curious moments is also a skill to keep your brain young.

Our each experience has two key ingredients: attention + interpretations. As we get older and familiar with the world around us, greater proportion of our experience is filled with interpretations. The curious moments practice invites you to fill your experience with greater attention, and delay interpretations.

The practice entails choosing to notice greater details in what might be mundane experience by assuming that nothing is ordinary and that everything around us is extremely novel and has details worth appreciating.

Here are a few starter details you can notice:
◊ Pick a flower and notice the arrangement of petals, the shape and markings on each petal, the central stamen, its stalk, the color pattern, and more.
◊ Examine your own hands and notice which finger is longer between pointer and ring finger. Compare the two hands.
◊ Walk around the neighborhood and see if you can find the stump of an old tree that you may have otherwise missed.
◊ Notice the logos of your favorite brands and try to memorize the details—text, color, shape, and overall design.
◊ At the airport or in a mall, notice that every person has a slightly different hairstyle.
◊ Fully get to know an apple or a water melon, noticing their color, the different markings, the surface texture, and more.

The curious moments practice is to notice at least one new detail every day.

If you wish you can partner with someone so you share the novelty you both noticed during the day. Partnering with children, encouraging them to notice one new details at the school and then letting them describe it at the end of the day, might not only provide a good starter topic for evening conversation, but also improve their attention.

A slight variant of this practice is the FOND practice – Fine One New Detail. In this practice, you are invited to pick a familiar object, such as your shirt or shoe. Examine this object until you find at least one detail you hadn't noticed before.

#4. Kind Attention: Our ancestors lived in small tribes that competed with each other for limited resources. Inter-tribal trust was low, conflicts were frequent. Our instincts at seeing a person from another tribe thus weren't of compassion and forgiveness. We looked out for threat, measured the stranger's strength and fighting ability. The problem is: even after the phenomenal technological and cultural progress and expanding our tribe size from 150 to millions (in a large city), we are still looking at each other with the same suspicion.

When we see a stranger, within about 30 milliseconds we make a quick judgment whether that person is trustworthy, attractive, and competent. Most of these judgments are instinctive and many aren't correct. Yet we keep doing it all day long. This can get exhausting on a busy day when you have to meet a lot of people. A more enriching alternate is kind attention.

Kind attention recognizes that every person in the world shares two distinct details with each other and with you: they are special (to someone), and they are struggling.

Kind attention thus remembers these two facts:
◊   Instinctive attention often judges others
◊   Most people are special and struggling

With this awareness, when you see people, instead of letting your instinctive attention judge them, remembering that they are special and struggling, send them a silent: I wish you well.

This is a silent intention. You don't have to say it. Also don't start it at places where you feel vulnerable. Practice this in your home, at a party, at the airport after the security check, in your office, at parent-teacher meeting, and more. This practice will connect you deeper with others, and give you better control over your emotions, particularly in a potentially adversarial meeting.

Further, when you send a silent good wish to others, you send a silent good wish to yourself. Kind attention is a very simple way to push away loneliness, uplift your emotions, and enhance your self-worth.

You can enhance this practice by becoming creative about how you apply it. A few ideas I have tried that have worked for me are:
- ◊ When flying above a city, send kind attention to every citizen living there.
- ◊ When you see an airliner in the sky, send kind attention to everyone sitting inside and wish them safe travels.
- ◊ When passing a pharmacy aisle, send kind attention to everyone who would be coming there today for buying medications to relieve their symptoms.
- ◊ When opening a door knob, send kind attention to everyone who held or will hold that door knob today.
- ◊ When trying to sleep at night, send kind attention to every parent who can't sleep tonight because they are tending to a sick child.

An easy way to integrate kind attention in your life is to practice a wishing well walk. Take a stroll in the mall, in your neighborhood, at your office, or some other place, and keep the intention of sending a silent good wish to as many people as you see. Let go of planning and problem solving in that time. I always come energized at the end of this walk.

The more creative you get about adding kindness to your life, the more opportunities you will find to help others feel worthy, in the process enhancing your own self-worth.

#5. Resilient Mindset: Each of the practices above is designed to
help you develop a deeper, focused, undistracted, and intentional attention. A strong attention will unfold your second core capacity—your ability to think intentional thoughts.

Our mind is a bit like an automobile. Just as you have to hold the steering wheel of your car, similarly, you have to hold the steering wheel of your mind. Personally, I can't trust my mind to think intentional and rational thoughts all the time. Every so often a thought emerges that I am embarrassed to own. A point came in my life when I realized that I need a set of principles to tether my thoughts. After much research and thinking I found five principles that I can trust and that are timeless. These are: gratitude, compassion, acceptance, meaning, and forgiveness.

Since five principles are too many to embody right away, I assigned each of them a day. The SMART program, in its initial phase follows the following sequence:
◊ Mondays are the days of gratitude
◊ Tuesdays are the days of compassion
◊ Wednesdays are the days of acceptance
◊ Thursdays are the days of meaning
◊ Fridays are the days of forgiveness

In case you are curious, Saturdays are the days of celebration, and Sundays are the days of reflection/prayer.

The purpose of assigning a day to each principle isn't meant to be too nerdy about it. You don't say I can't be compassionate on Thursdays since Tuesday is my day of compassion! The purpose is to give an initial anchor to your thoughts as you integrate these principles in your life. As your skills develop, you can pick any of the principles that makes the most sense to you at that time.

Resilient mindset invites you to integrate these five principles using one or more of the following ideas:
◊ **Read** about the principle—through one of the books including the books I have written (Mayo Clinic Guide to Stress-Free Living, Mayo Clinic Handbook for Happiness, Immerse: A 52-Week Course in Resilient Living, Mindfulness Redesigned for the Twenty-First Century), books of several other wonderful authors, online programs, and web search.
◊ **Think** about the principle—Think about what each principle means to you, how it can enhance your life, and how you can integrate the principle in your daily routine.
◊ **Write** about the principle—Write a journal, on paper or online. This journal provides you space to jot down your insights in brief. Please use additional pages as necessary.
◊ **Share** the principle—One of the strongest ways to bring the SMART concepts to your life is to buddy up with someone and mutually support your progress.
◊ **Practice** the principle—Find a way to practice the principle. Several ideas above will help you bring gratitude and compassion

(kindness) in your life. Acceptance, meaning, and forgiveness will need additional insights and I suggest you read more from one of the books I have suggested above or another book, to bring these timeless principles to your life.

Our overall goal is to lower our threshold for practicing the principles, so you do not wait for something phenomenal to feel grateful. You are grateful for a glass of clean water, a deep breath, a smile, a hello, and a hot shower. Similarly, you start seeing invisible suffering that afflicts almost everyone on our planet. In the process, you become kinder toward others and toward yourself. You stop being a visitor to the planet of kindness. You build that planet and live there.

The SMART Sequence

I suggest you bring the SMART skills to your life in two phases: Train and Sustain.

Train: The Train phase is generally four weeks long and roughly progresses in the following sequence:

	Week 1	Week 2	Week 3	Week 4
Morning Gratitude	✔	✔	✔	✔
The Two-Minute Rule		✔	✔	✔
Curious Moments		✔	✔	✔
Kind Attention			✔	✔
Resilient Mindset				✔

In other words:
- ◊ Start with morning gratitude for the first week
- ◊ Add the two-minute rule and/or curious moments in the second week
- ◊ Add kind attention in the third week
- ◊ Add resilient mindset in the fourth week
- ◊ From the fifth week onward customize the practices so they fit well with your life style and preferences

None of this is written in stone. If you find a slightly different way to bring these practices to your life or wish to start with the two-minute rule instead of morning gratitude, that will be totally fine.

Sustain: The sustain phase lasts your entire lifetime where you continue to deepen and broaden your skills. You continue customizing the skills to your life and sharing with others. If you wish, you are welcome to start a meditation practice such as calm and energize, rhythm, feelings, (all available on YouTube) or one of the other meditations available at myhappinesspal.com or other websites.

How to Use This Journal

The Resilience Journal invites you to interact with it twice a day for about two minutes. The journal offers four different ways you can interact with it:

#1. Set intention and asses action: First interaction with the journal generally is in the morning to set intention. Depending on how you anticipate your day, and your preference and finesse with the skills, you make a commitment to the specific skills you will practice by checking the appropriate boxes. Second interaction, generally at the end of day is to assess how well you did (assess action).

#2. Note your insights: At the end of each day you are invited to note any particular insight or observation you had during the day. This can pertain to your thoughts of gratitude and kindness, a particular observation, a unique connection you made, or anything else. I have purposefully chosen to keep it open to a variety of different ideas since if you picked just one theme (such as gratitude), then you might lose the novelty after some time.

#3. Creative Immersion: At the end of every two weeks, the journal invites you to explore deeper within yourself and in the outer world to nurture a healthier you, enhance your longevity, find inspiration, hope and courage, invite forgiveness and meaning, and thus live a more fulfilling life. We even focus on becoming better at multitasking and driving safer. I believe the combination of skills offered in this journal will help offer you a complete package to become kinder, stronger, and happier, on your path to achieving your highest potential.

#4 Resilience quote: Each page of the journal provides a resilience quote that is drawn from one of my previous books (mostly Mindfulness Redesigned). Most of the quotes are based on one or more research studies. I invite you to meditate on the ideas expressed and think about ways you can integrate the suggestions in your daily life.

Please note that as you try some of these practices, you don't have to be perfect each day. You will get bored, fail, disappoint yourself, and more. That's all just fine. Take it all in stride and keep moving forward. Further, some of the skills may not apply or resonate with you. Just omit them and choose the ones that make the most sense.

You'll notice that for the first day, the journal offers a brief recap of the individual practices. After that, the details are omitted and only the title of the practices are mentioned.

If you haven't done so far, I strongly suggest for you to read 'The Five SMART Skills' and 'The SMART Sequence' above. That'll help you get the maximum benefit from this journal.

I hope your journey into resilience is rewarding and truly lifts your entire life.

Thank you for trusting me with your time. Here is your resilience journal!

The Resilience Journal

Date: _____ / _____ / _____ Day 1

Practices	Set Intention Today I will practice the following (check all that apply):	Assess Action Today I was able to practice the following (check all that apply):
Morning Gratitude Think about and send silent gratitude to a few people in the morning before you get out of the bed.	☐	☐
The Two-Minute Rule Meet your family at the end of the day as if you haven't seen them for a month. Choose not to improve anyone in those two minutes. You can also practice this exercise with a friend, a colleague, a neighbor, a pet, or someone else.	☐	☐
Curious Moments Notice at least one new thing or one new detail today.	☐	☐
Kind Attention Assume most people you meet today are special and struggling. Send a silent good wish to as many as you can.	☐	☐

Resilience Thinking Align your thoughts with one or more of these five principles: Gratitude, Compassion, Acceptance, Meaning, Forgiveness.	Gratitude (Mon)	☐	
	Compassion (Tue)	☐	☐
	Acceptance (Wed)	☐	
	Meaning (Thu)	☐	
	Forgiveness (Fri)	☐	

An insight I learned today:_____

_____

People who make us feel unworthy occupy a disproportionate real estate in our head. Cancel their lease, at least for today.

Date: _____ / _____ / _____ Day _____

Practices	Set Intention	Assess Action
Morning Gratitude	☐	☐
The Two-Minute Rule	☐	☐
Curious Moments	☐	☐
Kind Attention	☐	☐
Resilience Thinking	☐	☐

An insight I learned today:_____

_____

Date: _____ / _____ / _____ Day _____

Practices	Set Intention	Assess Action
Morning Gratitude	☐	☐
The Two-Minute Rule	☐	☐
Curious Moments	☐	☐
Kind Attention	☐	☐
Resilience Thinking	☐	☐

An insight I learned today:_____

_____

Open your eyes & look up when the world wants you to shut your eyes & look down. The brightest stars appear on the darkest nights.

Date: _____ / _____ / _____ Day _____

Practices	Set Intention	Assess Action
Morning Gratitude	☐	☐
The Two-Minute Rule	☐	☐
Curious Moments	☐	☐
Kind Attention	☐	☐
Resilience Thinking	☐	☐

An insight I learned today:_____
_____

Date: _____ / _____ / _____ Day _____

Practices	Set Intention	Assess Action
Morning Gratitude	☐	☐
The Two-Minute Rule	☐	☐
Curious Moments	☐	☐
Kind Attention	☐	☐
Resilience Thinking	☐	☐

An insight I learned today:_____
_____

> How you drive is as important as where you are going. Perhaps you aren't going anywhere, just becoming a better driver.

Date: _____ / _____ / _____ Day _____

Practices	Set Intention	Assess Action
Morning Gratitude	☐	☐
The Two-Minute Rule	☐	☐
Curious Moments	☐	☐
Kind Attention	☐	☐
Resilience Thinking	☐	☐

An insight I learned today:_____

_____

Date: _____ / _____ / _____ Day _____

Practices	Set Intention	Assess Action
Morning Gratitude	☐	☐
The Two-Minute Rule	☐	☐
Curious Moments	☐	☐
Kind Attention	☐	☐
Resilience Thinking	☐	☐

An insight I learned today:_____

_____

Although we can't change our genetic sequence, we can influence which genes are expressed. And that may be enough.

Creative Immersion #1

Make a list of the people who are currently in your personal life and mean a lot to you.

_____   _____

_____   _____

_____   _____

_____   _____

Make a list of people who are currently in your professional life and mean a lot to you.

_____   _____

_____   _____

_____   _____

Make a list of people who have passed away who mean a lot to you.

_____   _____

_____   _____

_____   _____

Suggested activities for the next two weeks:

◊   Keep at least one person from the lists above in your morning gratitude practice.

◊   Pick an inspiring book you have been wanting to read for a long time. Try and read this book in the next two weeks.

Date: _____ / _____ / _____ Day _____

Practices	Set Intention	Assess Action
Morning Gratitude	☐	☐
The Two-Minute Rule	☐	☐
Curious Moments	☐	☐
Kind Attention	☐	☐
Resilience Thinking	☐	☐

An insight I learned today:_____

_____

Date: _____ / _____ / _____ Day _____

Practices	Set Intention	Assess Action
Morning Gratitude	☐	☐
The Two-Minute Rule	☐	☐
Curious Moments	☐	☐
Kind Attention	☐	☐
Resilience Thinking	☐	☐

An insight I learned today:_____

_____

> Courage is recognizing that the meaning that drives you is more powerful than the fears that hold you.

Date: _____ / _____ / _____ Day _____

Practices	Set Intention	Assess Action
Morning Gratitude	☐	☐
The Two-Minute Rule	☐	☐
Curious Moments	☐	☐
Kind Attention	☐	☐
Resilience Thinking	☐	☐

An insight I learned today:_____

_____

Date: _____ / _____ / _____ Day _____

Practices	Set Intention	Assess Action
Morning Gratitude	☐	☐
The Two-Minute Rule	☐	☐
Curious Moments	☐	☐
Kind Attention	☐	☐
Resilience Thinking	☐	☐

An insight I learned today:_____

_____

Hope doesn't mean it won't ever get dark. Hope means no matter how dark the night, the sun will always appear in the morning.

Date: _____ / _____ / _____ Day _____

Practices	Set Intention	Assess Action
Morning Gratitude	☐	☐
The Two-Minute Rule	☐	☐
Curious Moments	☐	☐
Kind Attention	☐	☐
Resilience Thinking	☐	☐

An insight I learned today:_____

_____

Date: _____ / _____ / _____ Day _____

Practices	Set Intention	Assess Action
Morning Gratitude	☐	☐
The Two-Minute Rule	☐	☐
Curious Moments	☐	☐
Kind Attention	☐	☐
Resilience Thinking	☐	☐

An insight I learned today:_____

_____

> Each undone task takes double the headspace compared to a completed task or one for which you have a plan.

Date: _____ / _____ / _____ Day _____

Practices	Set Intention	Assess Action
Morning Gratitude	☐	☐
The Two-Minute Rule	☐	☐
Curious Moments	☐	☐
Kind Attention	☐	☐
Resilience Thinking	☐	☐

An insight I learned today:_____

_____

Date: _____ / _____ / _____ Day _____

Practices	Set Intention	Assess Action
Morning Gratitude	☐	☐
The Two-Minute Rule	☐	☐
Curious Moments	☐	☐
Kind Attention	☐	☐
Resilience Thinking	☐	☐

An insight I learned today:_____

> Commit to doing something good, however small, each day. It will be the start of a transformation.

Date: _____ / _____ / _____ Day _____

Practices	Set Intention	Assess Action
Morning Gratitude	☐	☐
The Two-Minute Rule	☐	☐
Curious Moments	☐	☐
Kind Attention	☐	☐
Resilience Thinking	☐	☐

An insight I learned today:_____

_____

Date: _____ / _____ / _____ Day _____

Practices	Set Intention	Assess Action
Morning Gratitude	☐	☐
The Two-Minute Rule	☐	☐
Curious Moments	☐	☐
Kind Attention	☐	☐
Resilience Thinking	☐	☐

An insight I learned today:_____

_____

Gratitude & compassion are so beneficial that if they were a pill, we would be taking them three times a day & not mind the copay.

Date: _____ / _____ / _____ Day _____

Practices	Set Intention	Assess Action
Morning Gratitude	☐	☐
The Two-Minute Rule	☐	☐
Curious Moments	☐	☐
Kind Attention	☐	☐
Resilience Thinking	☐	☐

An insight I learned today:_____

_____

Date: _____ / _____ / _____ Day _____

Practices	Set Intention	Assess Action
Morning Gratitude	☐	☐
The Two-Minute Rule	☐	☐
Curious Moments	☐	☐
Kind Attention	☐	☐
Resilience Thinking	☐	☐

An insight I learned today:_____

_____

Just as a honeybee collects nectar from many flowers, collect wisdom from many role models.

Date: _____ / _____ / _____ Day _____

Practices	Set Intention	Assess Action
Morning Gratitude	☐	☐
The Two-Minute Rule	☐	☐
Curious Moments	☐	☐
Kind Attention	☐	☐
Resilience Thinking	☐	☐

An insight I learned today:_____

_____

Date: _____ / _____ / _____ Day _____

Practices	Set Intention	Assess Action
Morning Gratitude	☐	☐
The Two-Minute Rule	☐	☐
Curious Moments	☐	☐
Kind Attention	☐	☐
Resilience Thinking	☐	☐

An insight I learned today:_____

_____

Start your day assuming you are a phenomenal person. A bad thought, word, or action is unbecoming of you.

Creative Immersion #2

This is the book I read in the previous two weeks:

_____

The following are the top ten insights I learned from this book:

_____

_____

_____

_____

_____

_____

_____

_____

_____

_____

Research the physical effects of prolonged sitting and note them below.

_____   _____

_____   _____

_____   _____

Suggested activity for the next two weeks:
◊   Decrease your 'sitting time' (as you are able) during the day.

Date: _____ / _____ / _____ Day _____

Practices	Set Intention	Assess Action
Morning Gratitude	☐	☐
The Two-Minute Rule	☐	☐
Curious Moments	☐	☐
Kind Attention	☐	☐
Resilience Thinking	☐	☐

An insight I learned today:_____

_____

Date: _____ / _____ / _____ Day _____

Practices	Set Intention	Assess Action
Morning Gratitude	☐	☐
The Two-Minute Rule	☐	☐
Curious Moments	☐	☐
Kind Attention	☐	☐
Resilience Thinking	☐	☐

An insight I learned today:_____

_____

Forgiveness takes the power from the other person and empowers you to choose your mindset based on your values.

Date: _____ / _____ / _____ Day _____

Practices	Set Intention	Assess Action
Morning Gratitude	☐	☐
The Two-Minute Rule	☐	☐
Curious Moments	☐	☐
Kind Attention	☐	☐
Resilience Thinking	☐	☐

An insight I learned today:_____

_____

Date: _____ / _____ / _____ Day _____

Practices	Set Intention	Assess Action
Morning Gratitude	☐	☐
The Two-Minute Rule	☐	☐
Curious Moments	☐	☐
Kind Attention	☐	☐
Resilience Thinking	☐	☐

An insight I learned today:_____

_____

Acting superior is a reflection of feeling inferior. The hallmark of a phenomenal leader is his or her phenomenal humility.

Date: _____ / _____ / _____ Day _____

Practices	Set Intention	Assess Action
Morning Gratitude	☐	☐
The Two-Minute Rule	☐	☐
Curious Moments	☐	☐
Kind Attention	☐	☐
Resilience Thinking	☐	☐

An insight I learned today:_____

_____

Date: _____ / _____ / _____ Day _____

Practices	Set Intention	Assess Action
Morning Gratitude	☐	☐
The Two-Minute Rule	☐	☐
Curious Moments	☐	☐
Kind Attention	☐	☐
Resilience Thinking	☐	☐

An insight I learned today:_____

_____

In this world of infinite personalities and agendas, some people are bound to be allergic to you. Focus on the other eight billion.

Date: _____ / _____ / _____ Day _____

Practices	Set Intention	Assess Action
Morning Gratitude	☐	☐
The Two-Minute Rule	☐	☐
Curious Moments	☐	☐
Kind Attention	☐	☐
Resilience Thinking	☐	☐

An insight I learned today:_____

_____

Date: _____ / _____ / _____ Day _____

Practices	Set Intention	Assess Action
Morning Gratitude	☐	☐
The Two-Minute Rule	☐	☐
Curious Moments	☐	☐
Kind Attention	☐	☐
Resilience Thinking	☐	☐

An insight I learned today:_____

_____

Empty the space in your brain that is usurped by self-doubt. Replace it with hope, inspiration, and courage.

Date: _____ / _____ / _____ Day _____

Practices	Set Intention	Assess Action
Morning Gratitude	☐	☐
The Two-Minute Rule	☐	☐
Curious Moments	☐	☐
Kind Attention	☐	☐
Resilience Thinking	☐	☐

An insight I learned today:_____

_____

Date: _____ / _____ / _____ Day _____

Practices	Set Intention	Assess Action
Morning Gratitude	☐	☐
The Two-Minute Rule	☐	☐
Curious Moments	☐	☐
Kind Attention	☐	☐
Resilience Thinking	☐	☐

An insight I learned today:_____

_____

> If the world gets cold on you, you'll have to get tough and thick-skinned like the evergreens.

Date: _____ / _____ / _____ Day _____

Practices	Set Intention	Assess Action
Morning Gratitude	☐	☐
The Two-Minute Rule	☐	☐
Curious Moments	☐	☐
Kind Attention	☐	☐
Resilience Thinking	☐	☐

An insight I learned today:_____

_____

Date: _____ / _____ / _____ Day _____

Practices	Set Intention	Assess Action
Morning Gratitude	☐	☐
The Two-Minute Rule	☐	☐
Curious Moments	☐	☐
Kind Attention	☐	☐
Resilience Thinking	☐	☐

An insight I learned today:_____

_____

The good people are very good at feeling bad about themselves. If you've felt bad about yourself, it's a proof that you're a good person.

Date: _____ / _____ / _____ Day _____

Practices	Set Intention	Assess Action
Morning Gratitude	☐	☐
The Two-Minute Rule	☐	☐
Curious Moments	☐	☐
Kind Attention	☐	☐
Resilience Thinking	☐	☐

An insight I learned today:_____

_____

Date: _____ / _____ / _____ Day _____

Practices	Set Intention	Assess Action
Morning Gratitude	☐	☐
The Two-Minute Rule	☐	☐
Curious Moments	☐	☐
Kind Attention	☐	☐
Resilience Thinking	☐	☐

An insight I learned today:_____

_____

Birds with asymmetric feathers are the ones that can fly. Symmetry looks pretty, but sometimes life's asymmetries help us ascend.

Creative Immersion #3

How successful were you at decreasing your 'sitting time'?

1	2	3	4	5	6	7
Not at all						Completely

What benefits have you observed from decreasing your 'sitting time'?

_____

_____

_____

If you would like to further improve your physical activity, can you think of additional ideas about how you can become more active in the coming two weeks (feel free to research online)?

_____

_____

_____

_____

Suggested activities for the next two weeks:

◊ Find your four numbers—Cholesterol, blood sugar, blood pressure, and BMI. Research (using reliable resources) if your numbers are optimal and if not, what lifestyle and other changes you can do to improve them. You might need expert guidance for this.

◊ Continue working on decreasing your 'sitting time' for the next two weeks.

Date: _____ / _____ / _____ Day _____

Practices	Set Intention	Assess Action
Morning Gratitude	☐	☐
The Two-Minute Rule	☐	☐
Curious Moments	☐	☐
Kind Attention	☐	☐
Resilience Thinking	☐	☐

An insight I learned today:_____

_____

Date: _____ / _____ / _____ Day _____

Practices	Set Intention	Assess Action
Morning Gratitude	☐	☐
The Two-Minute Rule	☐	☐
Curious Moments	☐	☐
Kind Attention	☐	☐
Resilience Thinking	☐	☐

An insight I learned today:_____

_____

One of the best ways to be liked by others is to let them know that you like them.

Date: _____ / _____ / _____ Day _____

Practices	Set Intention	Assess Action
Morning Gratitude	☐	☐
The Two-Minute Rule	☐	☐
Curious Moments	☐	☐
Kind Attention	☐	☐
Resilience Thinking	☐	☐

An insight I learned today:_____

_____

Date: _____ / _____ / _____ Day _____

Practices	Set Intention	Assess Action
Morning Gratitude	☐	☐
The Two-Minute Rule	☐	☐
Curious Moments	☐	☐
Kind Attention	☐	☐
Resilience Thinking	☐	☐

An insight I learned today:_____

_____

With two-thirds of the earth covered with clouds, they will rain on you someday. You can't stop the rain but you can use the umbrella.

Date: _____ / _____ / _____ Day _____

Practices	Set Intention	Assess Action
Morning Gratitude	☐	☐
The Two-Minute Rule	☐	☐
Curious Moments	☐	☐
Kind Attention	☐	☐
Resilience Thinking	☐	☐

An insight I learned today:_____

_____

Date: _____ / _____ / _____ Day _____

Practices	Set Intention	Assess Action
Morning Gratitude	☐	☐
The Two-Minute Rule	☐	☐
Curious Moments	☐	☐
Kind Attention	☐	☐
Resilience Thinking	☐	☐

An insight I learned today:_____

_____

Allow only those things to bother you that will continue to bother you in five years. Look at the truth in its most optimistic version.

Date: _____ / _____ / _____ Day _____

Practices	Set Intention	Assess Action
Morning Gratitude	☐	☐
The Two-Minute Rule	☐	☐
Curious Moments	☐	☐
Kind Attention	☐	☐
Resilience Thinking	☐	☐

An insight I learned today:_____

_____

Date: _____ / _____ / _____ Day _____

Practices	Set Intention	Assess Action
Morning Gratitude	☐	☐
The Two-Minute Rule	☐	☐
Curious Moments	☐	☐
Kind Attention	☐	☐
Resilience Thinking	☐	☐

An insight I learned today:_____

_____

Hurry decimates quality and joy. Avoid time pressure by keeping your to-do list short & your not-to-do list long (as much as feasible).

Date: _____ / _____ / _____ Day _____

Practices	Set Intention	Assess Action
Morning Gratitude	☐	☐
The Two-Minute Rule	☐	☐
Curious Moments	☐	☐
Kind Attention	☐	☐
Resilience Thinking	☐	☐

An insight I learned today:_____

_____

Date: _____ / _____ / _____ Day _____

Practices	Set Intention	Assess Action
Morning Gratitude	☐	☐
The Two-Minute Rule	☐	☐
Curious Moments	☐	☐
Kind Attention	☐	☐
Resilience Thinking	☐	☐

An insight I learned today:_____

_____

Your effort and intentions and not the outcomes are in your control.
Peg your self-worth on effort and intentions, and not the outcomes.

Date: _____ / _____ / _____ Day _____

Practices	Set Intention	Assess Action
Morning Gratitude	☐	☐
The Two-Minute Rule	☐	☐
Curious Moments	☐	☐
Kind Attention	☐	☐
Resilience Thinking	☐	☐

An insight I learned today:_____

_____

Date: _____ / _____ / _____ Day _____

Practices	Set Intention	Assess Action
Morning Gratitude	☐	☐
The Two-Minute Rule	☐	☐
Curious Moments	☐	☐
Kind Attention	☐	☐
Resilience Thinking	☐	☐

An insight I learned today:_____

The dollars you earn isn't a barometer of your success. Your success is in the values you embody and the purpose you serve.

Date: _____ / _____ / _____ Day _____

Practices	Set Intention	Assess Action
Morning Gratitude	☐	☐
The Two-Minute Rule	☐	☐
Curious Moments	☐	☐
Kind Attention	☐	☐
Resilience Thinking	☐	☐

An insight I learned today:_____

_____

Date: _____ / _____ / _____ Day _____

Practices	Set Intention	Assess Action
Morning Gratitude	☐	☐
The Two-Minute Rule	☐	☐
Curious Moments	☐	☐
Kind Attention	☐	☐
Resilience Thinking	☐	☐

An insight I learned today:_____

_____

Revisit kind & happy memories by rethinking them often. Think more about people who lift your self-worth, not the ones who judge you.

Creative Immersion #4

Were you able to find your numbers?

Yes   No

If yes, is there room for improvement?

Yes   No

If yes, what actions are you willing to take to improve your numbers?
I am willing to_____

_____

_____

_____

Why do you care about being healthier?

I want to be healthier because_____

_____

_____

_____

Suggested activities for the next two weeks:
◊   Research one dish you haven't tried before that you find healthy, nourishing, and will likely soothe your palate (as in delicious!). Consider trying this dish in the next two weeks.

◊   Research the health and mood effects of watching too much news. If the findings concern you, consider decreasing your exposure to the news in the next two weeks.

Date: _____ / _____ / _____ Day _____

Practices	Set Intention	Assess Action
Morning Gratitude	☐	☐
The Two-Minute Rule	☐	☐
Curious Moments	☐	☐
Kind Attention	☐	☐
Resilience Thinking	☐	☐

An insight I learned today:_____

_____

Date: _____ / _____ / _____ Day _____

Practices	Set Intention	Assess Action
Morning Gratitude	☐	☐
The Two-Minute Rule	☐	☐
Curious Moments	☐	☐
Kind Attention	☐	☐
Resilience Thinking	☐	☐

An insight I learned today:_____

_____

When you get busy helping the world, the world gets busy helping you.
The world, however, is almost always slower than desirable.

Date: _____ / _____ / _____ Day _____

Practices	Set Intention	Assess Action
Morning Gratitude	☐	☐
The Two-Minute Rule	☐	☐
Curious Moments	☐	☐
Kind Attention	☐	☐
Resilience Thinking	☐	☐

An insight I learned today:_____

_____

Date: _____ / _____ / _____ Day _____

Practices	Set Intention	Assess Action
Morning Gratitude	☐	☐
The Two-Minute Rule	☐	☐
Curious Moments	☐	☐
Kind Attention	☐	☐
Resilience Thinking	☐	☐

An insight I learned today:_____

_____

Find novel within the familiar to keep your life interesting. Find familiar within the novel so you don't get overwhelmed.

Date: _____ / _____ / _____ Day _____

Practices	Set Intention	Assess Action
Morning Gratitude	☐	☐
The Two-Minute Rule	☐	☐
Curious Moments	☐	☐
Kind Attention	☐	☐
Resilience Thinking	☐	☐

An insight I learned today:_____

_____

Date: _____ / _____ / _____ Day _____

Practices	Set Intention	Assess Action
Morning Gratitude	☐	☐
The Two-Minute Rule	☐	☐
Curious Moments	☐	☐
Kind Attention	☐	☐
Resilience Thinking	☐	☐

An insight I learned today:_____

_____

Fill your past with gratitude not regrets, present with meaning not greed, and future with hope not fear.

Date: _____ / _____ / _____ Day _____

Practices	Set Intention	Assess Action
Morning Gratitude	☐	☐
The Two-Minute Rule	☐	☐
Curious Moments	☐	☐
Kind Attention	☐	☐
Resilience Thinking	☐	☐

An insight I learned today:_____

_____

Date: _____ / _____ / _____ Day _____

Practices	Set Intention	Assess Action
Morning Gratitude	☐	☐
The Two-Minute Rule	☐	☐
Curious Moments	☐	☐
Kind Attention	☐	☐
Resilience Thinking	☐	☐

An insight I learned today:_____

_____

> Internally accepting others as they are is an optimal first step to bring about a change in them.

Date: _____ / _____ / _____ Day _____

Practices	Set Intention	Assess Action
Morning Gratitude	☐	☐
The Two-Minute Rule	☐	☐
Curious Moments	☐	☐
Kind Attention	☐	☐
Resilience Thinking	☐	☐

An insight I learned today:_____

_____

Date: _____ / _____ / _____ Day _____

Practices	Set Intention	Assess Action
Morning Gratitude	☐	☐
The Two-Minute Rule	☐	☐
Curious Moments	☐	☐
Kind Attention	☐	☐
Resilience Thinking	☐	☐

An insight I learned today:_____

_____

Never let someone who shouldn't be in your story, write the title of the story.

Date: _____ / _____ / _____ Day _____

Practices	Set Intention	Assess Action
Morning Gratitude	☐	☐
The Two-Minute Rule	☐	☐
Curious Moments	☐	☐
Kind Attention	☐	☐
Resilience Thinking	☐	☐

An insight I learned today:_____

_____

Date: _____ / _____ / _____ Day _____

Practices	Set Intention	Assess Action
Morning Gratitude	☐	☐
The Two-Minute Rule	☐	☐
Curious Moments	☐	☐
Kind Attention	☐	☐
Resilience Thinking	☐	☐

An insight I learned today:_____

_____

Happier folks don't have more positive & less negative events. They pay more attention to positive & less attention to negative events.

Date: _____ / _____ / _____ Day _____

Practices	Set Intention	Assess Action
Morning Gratitude	☐	☐
The Two-Minute Rule	☐	☐
Curious Moments	☐	☐
Kind Attention	☐	☐
Resilience Thinking	☐	☐

An insight I learned today:_____

_____

Date: _____ / _____ / _____ Day _____

Practices	Set Intention	Assess Action
Morning Gratitude	☐	☐
The Two-Minute Rule	☐	☐
Curious Moments	☐	☐
Kind Attention	☐	☐
Resilience Thinking	☐	☐

An insight I learned today:_____

_____

Personal hurts multiply when we visit them too often; personal hurts heal when we tend to others who are hurting.

Creative Immersion #5

Were you able to cut down on the news?

Yes   No

If no, how do you propose cutting down on the news in the coming two weeks (assuming you agree with this suggestion)?

_____

_____

If yes, what benefits did you notice from this change?

Cutting down on the news helped me_____

_____

_____

In a few words describe how would you rate your sleep—both quality and quantity?

_____

_____

Suggested activities for the next two weeks:
- ◊ Research the benefits of mind-body practices such as meditation, deep breathing, prayer, tai chi, and yoga.

- ◊ At least once, practice the ten-minute meditation – Calm and Energize. (Type calm and energize + Sood in YouTube, or you can access it at this link - https://www.youtube.com/watch?v=IGDJjO6WEb8)

Date: _____ / _____ / _____ Day _____

Practices	Set Intention	Assess Action
Morning Gratitude	☐	☐
The Two-Minute Rule	☐	☐
Curious Moments	☐	☐
Kind Attention	☐	☐
Resilience Thinking	☐	☐

An insight I learned today:_____

_____

Date: _____ / _____ / _____ Day _____

Practices	Set Intention	Assess Action
Morning Gratitude	☐	☐
The Two-Minute Rule	☐	☐
Curious Moments	☐	☐
Kind Attention	☐	☐
Resilience Thinking	☐	☐

An insight I learned today:_____

_____

Technology that doesn't deepen relationships and kindness hurts us in the long term. Every entrepreneur's brain needs a heart.

Date: _____ / _____ / _____ Day _____

Practices	Set Intention	Assess Action
Morning Gratitude	☐	☐
The Two-Minute Rule	☐	☐
Curious Moments	☐	☐
Kind Attention	☐	☐
Resilience Thinking	☐	☐

An insight I learned today: _____

_____

Date: _____ / _____ / _____ Day _____

Practices	Set Intention	Assess Action
Morning Gratitude	☐	☐
The Two-Minute Rule	☐	☐
Curious Moments	☐	☐
Kind Attention	☐	☐
Resilience Thinking	☐	☐

An insight I learned today: _____

_____

Comparison can seed envy and hubris or inspiration and humility. The choice is yours.

Date: _____ / _____ / _____ Day _____

Practices	Set Intention	Assess Action
Morning Gratitude	☐	☐
The Two-Minute Rule	☐	☐
Curious Moments	☐	☐
Kind Attention	☐	☐
Resilience Thinking	☐	☐

An insight I learned today:_____

_____

Date: _____ / _____ / _____ Day _____

Practices	Set Intention	Assess Action
Morning Gratitude	☐	☐
The Two-Minute Rule	☐	☐
Curious Moments	☐	☐
Kind Attention	☐	☐
Resilience Thinking	☐	☐

An insight I learned today:_____

_____

Being tough doesn't mean becoming callous and uncaring. It means letting yourself cry and finding a smile as the tears dry.

Date: _____ / _____ / _____ Day _____

Practices	Set Intention	Assess Action
Morning Gratitude	☐	☐
The Two-Minute Rule	☐	☐
Curious Moments	☐	☐
Kind Attention	☐	☐
Resilience Thinking	☐	☐

An insight I learned today:_____

_____

Date: _____ / _____ / _____ Day _____

Practices	Set Intention	Assess Action
Morning Gratitude	☐	☐
The Two-Minute Rule	☐	☐
Curious Moments	☐	☐
Kind Attention	☐	☐
Resilience Thinking	☐	☐

An insight I learned today:_____

_____

When you are not flying the plane, let your brain rest in the airplane mode.

Date: _____ / _____ / _____ Day _____

Practices	Set Intention	Assess Action
Morning Gratitude	☐	☐
The Two-Minute Rule	☐	☐
Curious Moments	☐	☐
Kind Attention	☐	☐
Resilience Thinking	☐	☐

An insight I learned today:_____

_____

Date: _____ / _____ / _____ Day _____

Practices	Set Intention	Assess Action
Morning Gratitude	☐	☐
The Two-Minute Rule	☐	☐
Curious Moments	☐	☐
Kind Attention	☐	☐
Resilience Thinking	☐	☐

An insight I learned today:_____

_____

The joy of remembering a good deed is almost as strong the tenth time
as it is the first time.

Date: _____ / _____ / _____ Day _____

Practices	Set Intention	Assess Action
Morning Gratitude	☐	☐
The Two-Minute Rule	☐	☐
Curious Moments	☐	☐
Kind Attention	☐	☐
Resilience Thinking	☐	☐

An insight I learned today:_____

_____

Date: _____ / _____ / _____ Day _____

Practices	Set Intention	Assess Action
Morning Gratitude	☐	☐
The Two-Minute Rule	☐	☐
Curious Moments	☐	☐
Kind Attention	☐	☐
Resilience Thinking	☐	☐

An insight I learned today:_____

Forgiving someone at work improves your relationships at home.
Forgiving someone at home improves your performance at work.

Date: _____ / _____ / _____ Day _____

Practices	Set Intention	Assess Action
Morning Gratitude	☐	☐
The Two-Minute Rule	☐	☐
Curious Moments	☐	☐
Kind Attention	☐	☐
Resilience Thinking	☐	☐

An insight I learned today:_____

_____

Date: _____ / _____ / _____ Day _____

Practices	Set Intention	Assess Action
Morning Gratitude	☐	☐
The Two-Minute Rule	☐	☐
Curious Moments	☐	☐
Kind Attention	☐	☐
Resilience Thinking	☐	☐

An insight I learned today:_____

_____

I have never met a compassionate person who lacked competence.
When we preserve compassion, we preserve it all.

Creative Immersion #6

What benefits of mind-body practices (such as meditation), you find most compelling?

_____

_____

_____

What are the top two reasons you might not be able to add a mind-body practice in your daily routine?

_____

_____

How do you propose overcoming these impediments (assuming you are interested in a mind-body practice)?

_____

_____

Any additional technique you wish to try to relax your mind?

_____

_____

Suggested activities for the next two weeks:
- ◊ Research different aspects of sleep hygiene. Pick one element from the list that you aren't doing well and apply it to your life.
- ◊ Notice how well you are doing with your driving. Are you following the speed limits, maintaining your lane, avoiding cell phone use, never texting while driving, giving appropriate signals, anticipating errors from others, avoiding sharp turns and cutting across others, not tailgating, and not getting into road rage? Pick one area that you aren't doing well that you commit to improving in the next two weeks.

Date: _____ / _____ / _____ Day _____

Practices	Set Intention	Assess Action
Morning Gratitude	☐	☐
The Two-Minute Rule	☐	☐
Curious Moments	☐	☐
Kind Attention	☐	☐
Resilience Thinking	☐	☐

An insight I learned today:_____

_____

Date: _____ / _____ / _____ Day _____

Practices	Set Intention	Assess Action
Morning Gratitude	☐	☐
The Two-Minute Rule	☐	☐
Curious Moments	☐	☐
Kind Attention	☐	☐
Resilience Thinking	☐	☐

An insight I learned today:_____

_____

> Think of what made you happy before you learned to get sad. It will give you an idea of how to be happy again.

Date: _____ / _____ / _____ Day _____

Practices	Set Intention	Assess Action
Morning Gratitude	☐	☐
The Two-Minute Rule	☐	☐
Curious Moments	☐	☐
Kind Attention	☐	☐
Resilience Thinking	☐	☐

An insight I learned today:_____

_____

Date: _____ / _____ / _____ Day _____

Practices	Set Intention	Assess Action
Morning Gratitude	☐	☐
The Two-Minute Rule	☐	☐
Curious Moments	☐	☐
Kind Attention	☐	☐
Resilience Thinking	☐	☐

An insight I learned today:_____

_____

If we all think, speak, and behave the way we want our children to think, speak, and behave, the world will be a much better place.

Date: _____ / _____ / _____ Day _____

Practices	Set Intention	Assess Action
Morning Gratitude	☐	☐
The Two-Minute Rule	☐	☐
Curious Moments	☐	☐
Kind Attention	☐	☐
Resilience Thinking	☐	☐

An insight I learned today:_____

_____

Date: _____ / _____ / _____ Day _____

Practices	Set Intention	Assess Action
Morning Gratitude	☐	☐
The Two-Minute Rule	☐	☐
Curious Moments	☐	☐
Kind Attention	☐	☐
Resilience Thinking	☐	☐

An insight I learned today:_____

A million likes on social media are not match for a single loving trusting relationship.

Date: _____ / _____ / _____ Day _____

Practices	Set Intention	Assess Action
Morning Gratitude	☐	☐
The Two-Minute Rule	☐	☐
Curious Moments	☐	☐
Kind Attention	☐	☐
Resilience Thinking	☐	☐

An insight I learned today:_____

_____

Date: _____ / _____ / _____ Day _____

Practices	Set Intention	Assess Action
Morning Gratitude	☐	☐
The Two-Minute Rule	☐	☐
Curious Moments	☐	☐
Kind Attention	☐	☐
Resilience Thinking	☐	☐

An insight I learned today:_____

Believe in, and remind yourself of this powerful mantra each day: "I am enough. I have enough."

Date: _____ / _____ / _____ Day _____

Practices	Set Intention	Assess Action
Morning Gratitude	☐	☐
The Two-Minute Rule	☐	☐
Curious Moments	☐	☐
Kind Attention	☐	☐
Resilience Thinking	☐	☐

An insight I learned today:_____

_____

Date: _____ / _____ / _____ Day _____

Practices	Set Intention	Assess Action
Morning Gratitude	☐	☐
The Two-Minute Rule	☐	☐
Curious Moments	☐	☐
Kind Attention	☐	☐
Resilience Thinking	☐	☐

An insight I learned today:_____

_____

> The courageous are good at managing fear. Courage is related more to the strength of the purpose than the power of the biceps.

Date: _____ / _____ / _____ Day _____

Practices	Set Intention	Assess Action
Morning Gratitude	☐	☐
The Two-Minute Rule	☐	☐
Curious Moments	☐	☐
Kind Attention	☐	☐
Resilience Thinking	☐	☐

An insight I learned today:_____

_____

Date: _____ / _____ / _____ Day _____

Practices	Set Intention	Assess Action
Morning Gratitude	☐	☐
The Two-Minute Rule	☐	☐
Curious Moments	☐	☐
Kind Attention	☐	☐
Resilience Thinking	☐	☐

An insight I learned today:_____

_____

Fill your past with gratitude not regrets, present with meaning not greed, and future with hope not fear.

Date: _____ / _____ / _____ Day _____

Practices	Set Intention	Assess Action
Morning Gratitude	☐	☐
The Two-Minute Rule	☐	☐
Curious Moments	☐	☐
Kind Attention	☐	☐
Resilience Thinking	☐	☐

An insight I learned today:_____

_____

Date: _____ / _____ / _____ Day _____

Practices	Set Intention	Assess Action
Morning Gratitude	☐	☐
The Two-Minute Rule	☐	☐
Curious Moments	☐	☐
Kind Attention	☐	☐
Resilience Thinking	☐	☐

An insight I learned today:_____

Others value you not as you are but as they are. Giving them the power to influence your self-worth is giving away too much control.

Creative Immersion #7

Were you able to at least slightly improve your sleep?
Yes   No

If yes, what benefits did you notice from this change?

Improving my sleep helped me_____

_____

_____

Were you able to at least slightly improve your driving?
Yes   No

If yes, what benefits did you notice from this change?

Improving my driving helped me_____

_____
How do you propose to keep working on your sleep and your driving?
Sleep:_____

Driving:_____

Suggested activities for the next two weeks:
  ◊   Make a list of three people who inspire you—one you
      personally know, and two national or international figures.

_____   _____   _____

  ◊   Research positive attributes of the people who inspire you.

Date: _____ / _____ / _____ Day _____

Practices	Set Intention	Assess Action
Morning Gratitude	☐	☐
The Two-Minute Rule	☐	☐
Curious Moments	☐	☐
Kind Attention	☐	☐
Resilience Thinking	☐	☐

An insight I learned today:_____

_____

Date: _____ / _____ / _____ Day _____

Practices	Set Intention	Assess Action
Morning Gratitude	☐	☐
The Two-Minute Rule	☐	☐
Curious Moments	☐	☐
Kind Attention	☐	☐
Resilience Thinking	☐	☐

An insight I learned today:_____

_____

A candle has to burn to light up the room. You'll have to endure some pain to bring light to people's lives.

Date: _____ / _____ / _____ Day _____

Practices	Set Intention	Assess Action
Morning Gratitude	☐	☐
The Two-Minute Rule	☐	☐
Curious Moments	☐	☐
Kind Attention	☐	☐
Resilience Thinking	☐	☐

An insight I learned today:_____

_____

Date: _____ / _____ / _____ Day _____

Practices	Set Intention	Assess Action
Morning Gratitude	☐	☐
The Two-Minute Rule	☐	☐
Curious Moments	☐	☐
Kind Attention	☐	☐
Resilience Thinking	☐	☐

An insight I learned today:_____

_____

Believe in those who believe in you. You are who your pet thinks you are.

Date: _____ / _____ / _____ Day _____

Practices	Set Intention	Assess Action
Morning Gratitude	☐	☐
The Two-Minute Rule	☐	☐
Curious Moments	☐	☐
Kind Attention	☐	☐
Resilience Thinking	☐	☐

An insight I learned today:_____

_____

Date: _____ / _____ / _____ Day _____

Practices	Set Intention	Assess Action
Morning Gratitude	☐	☐
The Two-Minute Rule	☐	☐
Curious Moments	☐	☐
Kind Attention	☐	☐
Resilience Thinking	☐	☐

An insight I learned today:_____

_____

Forgive in honor of those who were hurt worse than you, yet still chose to forgive.

Date: _____ / _____ / _____ Day _____

Practices	Set Intention	Assess Action
Morning Gratitude	☐	☐
The Two-Minute Rule	☐	☐
Curious Moments	☐	☐
Kind Attention	☐	☐
Resilience Thinking	☐	☐

An insight I learned today:_____

_____

Date: _____ / _____ / _____ Day _____

Practices	Set Intention	Assess Action
Morning Gratitude	☐	☐
The Two-Minute Rule	☐	☐
Curious Moments	☐	☐
Kind Attention	☐	☐
Resilience Thinking	☐	☐

An insight I learned today:_____

_____

Sometimes a hurt hurled at us is other person's misguided efforts
toward self-protection.

Date: _____ / _____ / _____ Day _____

Practices	Set Intention	Assess Action
Morning Gratitude	☐	☐
The Two-Minute Rule	☐	☐
Curious Moments	☐	☐
Kind Attention	☐	☐
Resilience Thinking	☐	☐

An insight I learned today:_____

_____

Date: _____ / _____ / _____ Day _____

Practices	Set Intention	Assess Action
Morning Gratitude	☐	☐
The Two-Minute Rule	☐	☐
Curious Moments	☐	☐
Kind Attention	☐	☐
Resilience Thinking	☐	☐

An insight I learned today:_____

_____

Most people handle future adversity much better than they imagined.
So best to use your energy to prepare and not fear.

Date: _____ / _____ / _____ Day _____

Practices	Set Intention	Assess Action
Morning Gratitude	☐	☐
The Two-Minute Rule	☐	☐
Curious Moments	☐	☐
Kind Attention	☐	☐
Resilience Thinking	☐	☐

An insight I learned today:_____

_____

Date: _____ / _____ / _____ Day _____

Practices	Set Intention	Assess Action
Morning Gratitude	☐	☐
The Two-Minute Rule	☐	☐
Curious Moments	☐	☐
Kind Attention	☐	☐
Resilience Thinking	☐	☐

An insight I learned today:_____

_____

Impatience slows progress & accelerates aging. Practice patience in daily life. Sometimes load the dishwasher as if it were a jewelry box.

Date: _____ / _____ / _____ Day _____

Practices	Set Intention	Assess Action
Morning Gratitude	☐	☐
The Two-Minute Rule	☐	☐
Curious Moments	☐	☐
Kind Attention	☐	☐
Resilience Thinking	☐	☐

An insight I learned today:_____

_____

Date: _____ / _____ / _____ Day _____

Practices	Set Intention	Assess Action
Morning Gratitude	☐	☐
The Two-Minute Rule	☐	☐
Curious Moments	☐	☐
Kind Attention	☐	☐
Resilience Thinking	☐	☐

An insight I learned today:_____

The best way to be happy is to be a source of happiness. The best way to be a source of happiness is to seek it for someone else.

Creative Immersion #8

What are the top few positive attributes of the three people who inspire you?

Person #1. Name:_____

Positive attributes:_____

_____

Person #2. Name:_____

Positive attributes:_____

_____

Person #2. Name:_____

Positive attributes:_____

_____

Does the above list inspire you to make a change in your life? If yes, what is it?

_____

_____

Suggested activities for the next two weeks:
◊   Research the benefits and harms of multitasking.

◊   For the next two weeks, avoid multitasking while driving (and in situations that demand your full attention to be safe) and when talking to people.

Date: _____ / _____ / _____ Day _____

Practices	Set Intention	Assess Action
Morning Gratitude	☐	☐
The Two-Minute Rule	☐	☐
Curious Moments	☐	☐
Kind Attention	☐	☐
Resilience Thinking	☐	☐

An insight I learned today:_____

_____

Date: _____ / _____ / _____ Day _____

Practices	Set Intention	Assess Action
Morning Gratitude	☐	☐
The Two-Minute Rule	☐	☐
Curious Moments	☐	☐
Kind Attention	☐	☐
Resilience Thinking	☐	☐

An insight I learned today:_____

_____

> Resilience is a combination of strength and flexibility. Be flexible about the preferences and strong about the principles.

Date: _____ / _____ / _____ Day _____

Practices	Set Intention	Assess Action
Morning Gratitude	☐	☐
The Two-Minute Rule	☐	☐
Curious Moments	☐	☐
Kind Attention	☐	☐
Resilience Thinking	☐	☐

An insight I learned today:_____

_____

Date: _____ / _____ / _____ Day _____

Practices	Set Intention	Assess Action
Morning Gratitude	☐	☐
The Two-Minute Rule	☐	☐
Curious Moments	☐	☐
Kind Attention	☐	☐
Resilience Thinking	☐	☐

An insight I learned today:_____

_____

You are an agent of service and love, helping build a kinder and happier world for our planet's children.

Date: _____ / _____ / _____ Day _____

Practices	Set Intention	Assess Action
Morning Gratitude	☐	☐
The Two-Minute Rule	☐	☐
Curious Moments	☐	☐
Kind Attention	☐	☐
Resilience Thinking	☐	☐

An insight I learned today:_____

_____

Date: _____ / _____ / _____ Day _____

Practices	Set Intention	Assess Action
Morning Gratitude	☐	☐
The Two-Minute Rule	☐	☐
Curious Moments	☐	☐
Kind Attention	☐	☐
Resilience Thinking	☐	☐

An insight I learned today:_____

_____

As you shovel the snow, remember that snow is the water that you'll get to drink in the summer.

Date: _____ / _____ / _____ Day _____

Practices	Set Intention	Assess Action
Morning Gratitude	☐	☐
The Two-Minute Rule	☐	☐
Curious Moments	☐	☐
Kind Attention	☐	☐
Resilience Thinking	☐	☐

An insight I learned today:_____

_____

Date: _____ / _____ / _____ Day _____

Practices	Set Intention	Assess Action
Morning Gratitude	☐	☐
The Two-Minute Rule	☐	☐
Curious Moments	☐	☐
Kind Attention	☐	☐
Resilience Thinking	☐	☐

An insight I learned today:_____

_____

> We stop being miserable the day we decide to live our life helping others. We are because we belong.

Date: _____ / _____ / _____ Day _____

Practices	Set Intention	Assess Action
Morning Gratitude	☐	☐
The Two-Minute Rule	☐	☐
Curious Moments	☐	☐
Kind Attention	☐	☐
Resilience Thinking	☐	☐

An insight I learned today:_____

_____

Date: _____ / _____ / _____ Day _____

Practices	Set Intention	Assess Action
Morning Gratitude	☐	☐
The Two-Minute Rule	☐	☐
Curious Moments	☐	☐
Kind Attention	☐	☐
Resilience Thinking	☐	☐

An insight I learned today:_____

_____

Fear blocks self-destructive courage, while courage checks paralyzing fear. We need both fear and courage, in balance.

Date: _____ / _____ / _____ Day _____

Practices	Set Intention	Assess Action
Morning Gratitude	☐	☐
The Two-Minute Rule	☐	☐
Curious Moments	☐	☐
Kind Attention	☐	☐
Resilience Thinking	☐	☐

An insight I learned today:_____

_____

Date: _____ / _____ / _____ Day _____

Practices	Set Intention	Assess Action
Morning Gratitude	☐	☐
The Two-Minute Rule	☐	☐
Curious Moments	☐	☐
Kind Attention	☐	☐
Resilience Thinking	☐	☐

An insight I learned today:_____

_____

Find novelty within the familiar to keep life interesting and familiarity within the novel so you don't get overwhelmed.

Date: _____ / _____ / _____ Day _____

Practices	Set Intention	Assess Action
Morning Gratitude	☐	☐
The Two-Minute Rule	☐	☐
Curious Moments	☐	☐
Kind Attention	☐	☐
Resilience Thinking	☐	☐

An insight I learned today:_____

_____

Date: _____ / _____ / _____ Day _____

Practices	Set Intention	Assess Action
Morning Gratitude	☐	☐
The Two-Minute Rule	☐	☐
Curious Moments	☐	☐
Kind Attention	☐	☐
Resilience Thinking	☐	☐

An insight I learned today:_____

_____

The light you bring in the life of others simultaneously illuminates your own life.

Creative Immersion #9

Notice some observations on your experiment with decreasing multitasking.

_____

_____

_____

_____

How do you define hope?_____

_____

_____

What in your view are some of the benefits of being more hopeful?

_____

_____

_____

_____

Suggested activities for the next two weeks:
◊   Research some benefits of being more hopeful/optimistic. Find different ways of increasing hope and implement one or two strategies.

◊   Research different beliefs, practices, and lifestyle approaches that can increase your life span (hint—being hopeful/optimistic is one of them!).

Date: ____ / ____ / _____ Day _____

Practices	Set Intention	Assess Action
Morning Gratitude	☐	☐
The Two-Minute Rule	☐	☐
Curious Moments	☐	☐
Kind Attention	☐	☐
Resilience Thinking	☐	☐

An insight I learned today:_____

_____

Date: ____ / ____ / _____ Day _____

Practices	Set Intention	Assess Action
Morning Gratitude	☐	☐
The Two-Minute Rule	☐	☐
Curious Moments	☐	☐
Kind Attention	☐	☐
Resilience Thinking	☐	☐

An insight I learned today:_____

_____

On the road and in life, do not drive looking into the rear-view mirror all the time.

Date: _____ / _____ / _____ Day _____

Practices	Set Intention	Assess Action
Morning Gratitude	☐	☐
The Two-Minute Rule	☐	☐
Curious Moments	☐	☐
Kind Attention	☐	☐
Resilience Thinking	☐	☐

An insight I learned today:_____

_____

Date: _____ / _____ / _____ Day _____

Practices	Set Intention	Assess Action
Morning Gratitude	☐	☐
The Two-Minute Rule	☐	☐
Curious Moments	☐	☐
Kind Attention	☐	☐
Resilience Thinking	☐	☐

An insight I learned today:_____

_____

Forgiveness heals the past, lifts the present, and brightens the future.

Date: _____ / _____ / _____ Day _____

Practices	Set Intention	Assess Action
Morning Gratitude	☐	☐
The Two-Minute Rule	☐	☐
Curious Moments	☐	☐
Kind Attention	☐	☐
Resilience Thinking	☐	☐

An insight I learned today:_____

_____

Date: _____ / _____ / _____ Day _____

Practices	Set Intention	Assess Action
Morning Gratitude	☐	☐
The Two-Minute Rule	☐	☐
Curious Moments	☐	☐
Kind Attention	☐	☐
Resilience Thinking	☐	☐

An insight I learned today:_____

_____

It takes greater courage to forgive than to take revenge. Such courage ensures you end your life with fewer regrets.

Date: _____ / _____ / _____ Day _____

Practices	Set Intention	Assess Action
Morning Gratitude	☐	☐
The Two-Minute Rule	☐	☐
Curious Moments	☐	☐
Kind Attention	☐	☐
Resilience Thinking	☐	☐

An insight I learned today:_____

_____

Date: _____ / _____ / _____ Day _____

Practices	Set Intention	Assess Action
Morning Gratitude	☐	☐
The Two-Minute Rule	☐	☐
Curious Moments	☐	☐
Kind Attention	☐	☐
Resilience Thinking	☐	☐

An insight I learned today:_____

_____

Investing 101: A stock you purchase will always go down; a stock you sell will always go up.

Date: _____ / _____ / _____ Day _____

Practices	Set Intention	Assess Action
Morning Gratitude	☐	☐
The Two-Minute Rule	☐	☐
Curious Moments	☐	☐
Kind Attention	☐	☐
Resilience Thinking	☐	☐

An insight I learned today:_____

_____

Date: _____ / _____ / _____ Day _____

Practices	Set Intention	Assess Action
Morning Gratitude	☐	☐
The Two-Minute Rule	☐	☐
Curious Moments	☐	☐
Kind Attention	☐	☐
Resilience Thinking	☐	☐

An insight I learned today:_____

_____

Forgive yourself, if you don't have a PhD in human relationships and life's struggles, which none of us does.

Date: _____ / _____ / _____ Day _____

Practices	Set Intention	Assess Action
Morning Gratitude	☐	☐
The Two-Minute Rule	☐	☐
Curious Moments	☐	☐
Kind Attention	☐	☐
Resilience Thinking	☐	☐

An insight I learned today:_____

_____

Date: _____ / _____ / _____ Day _____

Practices	Set Intention	Assess Action
Morning Gratitude	☐	☐
The Two-Minute Rule	☐	☐
Curious Moments	☐	☐
Kind Attention	☐	☐
Resilience Thinking	☐	☐

An insight I learned today:_____

_____

Happiness = Reality – Expectations

Date: _____ / _____ / _____ Day _____

Practices	Set Intention	Assess Action
Morning Gratitude	☐	☐
The Two-Minute Rule	☐	☐
Curious Moments	☐	☐
Kind Attention	☐	☐
Resilience Thinking	☐	☐

An insight I learned today:_____

_____

Date: _____ / _____ / _____ Day _____

Practices	Set Intention	Assess Action
Morning Gratitude	☐	☐
The Two-Minute Rule	☐	☐
Curious Moments	☐	☐
Kind Attention	☐	☐
Resilience Thinking	☐	☐

An insight I learned today:_____

Assume everyone is phenomenally interesting and precious. See them in their circle of love.

Creative Immersion #10

List the beliefs, practices, and lifestyle approaches you have found that can increase your lifespan.

_____

_____

_____

_____

_____

Among the approaches mentioned above which ones are a low-hanging fruit for you?

_____

_____

What might be the next best step to practice one approach you listed above?

_____

_____

_____

Suggested activities for the next two weeks:
- ◊ Research the concept of courage—what is it, what are its benefits, and what are different ways to be more courageous?

- ◊ Watch a movie that shows the real-life experiences of a courageous person you admire.

Date: _____ / _____ / _____ Day _____

Practices	Set Intention	Assess Action
Morning Gratitude	☐	☐
The Two-Minute Rule	☐	☐
Curious Moments	☐	☐
Kind Attention	☐	☐
Resilience Thinking	☐	☐

An insight I learned today:_____

_____

Date: _____ / _____ / _____ Day _____

Practices	Set Intention	Assess Action
Morning Gratitude	☐	☐
The Two-Minute Rule	☐	☐
Curious Moments	☐	☐
Kind Attention	☐	☐
Resilience Thinking	☐	☐

An insight I learned today:_____

_____

> Our genes influence 50 percent of our personality that none of us get to choose. Think about this before judging yourself or others.

Date: _____ / _____ / _____ Day _____

Practices	Set Intention	Assess Action
Morning Gratitude	☐	☐
The Two-Minute Rule	☐	☐
Curious Moments	☐	☐
Kind Attention	☐	☐
Resilience Thinking	☐	☐

An insight I learned today:_____

_____

Date: _____ / _____ / _____ Day _____

Practices	Set Intention	Assess Action
Morning Gratitude	☐	☐
The Two-Minute Rule	☐	☐
Curious Moments	☐	☐
Kind Attention	☐	☐
Resilience Thinking	☐	☐

An insight I learned today:_____

_____

Do not discount the compliments that come your way. We tend to trust the criticism but disown the compliments.

Date: _____ / _____ / _____ Day _____

Practices	Set Intention	Assess Action
Morning Gratitude	☐	☐
The Two-Minute Rule	☐	☐
Curious Moments	☐	☐
Kind Attention	☐	☐
Resilience Thinking	☐	☐

An insight I learned today:_____

_____

Date: _____ / _____ / _____ Day _____

Practices	Set Intention	Assess Action
Morning Gratitude	☐	☐
The Two-Minute Rule	☐	☐
Curious Moments	☐	☐
Kind Attention	☐	☐
Resilience Thinking	☐	☐

An insight I learned today:_____

_____

Resist the urge to immediately provide insight to someone hurting.
Instead, provide validation, connection, support, and love.

Date: _____ / _____ / _____ Day _____

Practices	Set Intention	Assess Action
Morning Gratitude	☐	☐
The Two-Minute Rule	☐	☐
Curious Moments	☐	☐
Kind Attention	☐	☐
Resilience Thinking	☐	☐

An insight I learned today:_____

_____

Date: _____ / _____ / _____ Day _____

Practices	Set Intention	Assess Action
Morning Gratitude	☐	☐
The Two-Minute Rule	☐	☐
Curious Moments	☐	☐
Kind Attention	☐	☐
Resilience Thinking	☐	☐

An insight I learned today:_____

_____

Carefully choose which battles you wish to fight. The world will send you the size of the battles you choose to fight.

Date: _____ / _____ / _____ Day _____

Practices	Set Intention	Assess Action
Morning Gratitude	☐	☐
The Two-Minute Rule	☐	☐
Curious Moments	☐	☐
Kind Attention	☐	☐
Resilience Thinking	☐	☐

An insight I learned today:_____

_____

Date: _____ / _____ / _____ Day _____

Practices	Set Intention	Assess Action
Morning Gratitude	☐	☐
The Two-Minute Rule	☐	☐
Curious Moments	☐	☐
Kind Attention	☐	☐
Resilience Thinking	☐	☐

An insight I learned today:_____

_____

Feeling superior or feeling inferior, both make us vulnerable. The greatest joy is in feeling equal.

Date: _____ / _____ / _____ Day _____

Practices	Set Intention	Assess Action
Morning Gratitude	☐	☐
The Two-Minute Rule	☐	☐
Curious Moments	☐	☐
Kind Attention	☐	☐
Resilience Thinking	☐	☐

An insight I learned today:_____

_____

Date: _____ / _____ / _____ Day _____

Practices	Set Intention	Assess Action
Morning Gratitude	☐	☐
The Two-Minute Rule	☐	☐
Curious Moments	☐	☐
Kind Attention	☐	☐
Resilience Thinking	☐	☐

An insight I learned today:_____

_____

In our pursuit of happiness, material wealth is a much less efficient solution than boosting compassion for others and self.

Date: _____ / _____ / _____ Day _____

Practices	Set Intention	Assess Action
Morning Gratitude	☐	☐
The Two-Minute Rule	☐	☐
Curious Moments	☐	☐
Kind Attention	☐	☐
Resilience Thinking	☐	☐

An insight I learned today:_____
_____

Date: _____ / _____ / _____ Day _____

Practices	Set Intention	Assess Action
Morning Gratitude	☐	☐
The Two-Minute Rule	☐	☐
Curious Moments	☐	☐
Kind Attention	☐	☐
Resilience Thinking	☐	☐

An insight I learned today:_____

Patients being cared by more compassionate physicians have shorter duration of illness and better immune response.

Creative Immersion #11

Define courage.

_____

_____

What are some of the benefits of being courageous?

_____

_____

_____

How can one become more courageous?

_____

_____

_____

What might be the next best step for you to become more courageous?

_____

_____

_____

Suggested activities for the next two weeks:
- ◊ Research the benefit of having a strong sense of meaning to one's life?

- ◊ Think about what gives your life the greatest meaning?

Date: _____ / _____ / _____ Day _____

Practices	Set Intention	Assess Action
Morning Gratitude	☐	☐
The Two-Minute Rule	☐	☐
Curious Moments	☐	☐
Kind Attention	☐	☐
Resilience Thinking	☐	☐

An insight I learned today:_____

_____

Date: _____ / _____ / _____ Day _____

Practices	Set Intention	Assess Action
Morning Gratitude	☐	☐
The Two-Minute Rule	☐	☐
Curious Moments	☐	☐
Kind Attention	☐	☐
Resilience Thinking	☐	☐

An insight I learned today:_____

_____

Fifty percent of your impatience is encoded in your genes. Blame your genes for your impatience, pat your back for your patience!

Date: _____ / _____ / _____ Day _____

Practices	Set Intention	Assess Action
Morning Gratitude	☐	☐
The Two-Minute Rule	☐	☐
Curious Moments	☐	☐
Kind Attention	☐	☐
Resilience Thinking	☐	☐

An insight I learned today:_____

_____

Date: _____ / _____ / _____ Day _____

Practices	Set Intention	Assess Action
Morning Gratitude	☐	☐
The Two-Minute Rule	☐	☐
Curious Moments	☐	☐
Kind Attention	☐	☐
Resilience Thinking	☐	☐

An insight I learned today:_____

_____

Your CV will help you grow professionally, your eulogy will help you grow as a human being. Develop both through your earthly journey.

Date: _____ / _____ / _____ Day _____

Practices	Set Intention	Assess Action
Morning Gratitude	☐	☐
The Two-Minute Rule	☐	☐
Curious Moments	☐	☐
Kind Attention	☐	☐
Resilience Thinking	☐	☐

An insight I learned today:_____

_____

Date: _____ / _____ / _____ Day _____

Practices	Set Intention	Assess Action
Morning Gratitude	☐	☐
The Two-Minute Rule	☐	☐
Curious Moments	☐	☐
Kind Attention	☐	☐
Resilience Thinking	☐	☐

An insight I learned today:_____

_____

This too shall pass and it could have been much worse.

Date: _____ / _____ / _____ Day _____

Practices	Set Intention	Assess Action
Morning Gratitude	☐	☐
The Two-Minute Rule	☐	☐
Curious Moments	☐	☐
Kind Attention	☐	☐
Resilience Thinking	☐	☐

An insight I learned today:_____

_____

Date: _____ / _____ / _____ Day _____

Practices	Set Intention	Assess Action
Morning Gratitude	☐	☐
The Two-Minute Rule	☐	☐
Curious Moments	☐	☐
Kind Attention	☐	☐
Resilience Thinking	☐	☐

An insight I learned today:_____

_____

Grace is like sunlight, it illuminates every corner. But it is up to us to open the windows.

Date: _____ / _____ / _____ Day _____

Practices	Set Intention	Assess Action
Morning Gratitude	☐	☐
The Two-Minute Rule	☐	☐
Curious Moments	☐	☐
Kind Attention	☐	☐
Resilience Thinking	☐	☐

An insight I learned today:_____

_____

Date: _____ / _____ / _____ Day _____

Practices	Set Intention	Assess Action
Morning Gratitude	☐	☐
The Two-Minute Rule	☐	☐
Curious Moments	☐	☐
Kind Attention	☐	☐
Resilience Thinking	☐	☐

An insight I learned today:_____

_____

Courage keeps the company of humility. For their heroic deeds, the courageous often say, "I was just doing my job."

Date: _____ / _____ / _____ Day _____

Practices	Set Intention	Assess Action
Morning Gratitude	☐	☐
The Two-Minute Rule	☐	☐
Curious Moments	☐	☐
Kind Attention	☐	☐
Resilience Thinking	☐	☐

An insight I learned today:_____

_____

Date: _____ / _____ / _____ Day _____

Practices	Set Intention	Assess Action
Morning Gratitude	☐	☐
The Two-Minute Rule	☐	☐
Curious Moments	☐	☐
Kind Attention	☐	☐
Resilience Thinking	☐	☐

An insight I learned today:_____

_____

On a material level & for the short term, the world isn't fair. Bad things happen to good people, & good things happen to bad people.

Date: _____ / _____ / _____ Day _____

Practices	Set Intention	Assess Action
Morning Gratitude	☐	☐
The Two-Minute Rule	☐	☐
Curious Moments	☐	☐
Kind Attention	☐	☐
Resilience Thinking	☐	☐

An insight I learned today:_____

_____

Date: _____ / _____ / _____ Day _____

Practices	Set Intention	Assess Action
Morning Gratitude	☐	☐
The Two-Minute Rule	☐	☐
Curious Moments	☐	☐
Kind Attention	☐	☐
Resilience Thinking	☐	☐

An insight I learned today:_____

Forgiving can be very difficult. Forgetting is near impossible. Be kind to yourself in your journey into forgiveness.

Creative Immersion #12

How do you conceptualize meaning?

What are the benefits of having a strong sense of meaning?

What gives your life the greatest meaning?

What might be the next best steps for you to align your everyday activities with your higher meaning?

Suggested activities for the next two weeks:
- ◊ Research what is forgiveness.
- ◊ Research the benefits of forgiveness—on physical and mental health, and relationships.
- ◊ Ask this of yourself: Do I have anyone I need to forgive?

Date: _____ / _____ / _____ Day _____

Practices	Set Intention	Assess Action
Morning Gratitude	☐	☐
The Two-Minute Rule	☐	☐
Curious Moments	☐	☐
Kind Attention	☐	☐
Resilience Thinking	☐	☐

An insight I learned today:_____

_____

Date: _____ / _____ / _____ Day _____

Practices	Set Intention	Assess Action
Morning Gratitude	☐	☐
The Two-Minute Rule	☐	☐
Curious Moments	☐	☐
Kind Attention	☐	☐
Resilience Thinking	☐	☐

An insight I learned today:_____

_____

Increasing good thoughts is easier than eliminating the bad ones.
Crowd your mind and life with the good. The bad will slowly fade.

Date: _____ / _____ / _____ Day _____

Practices	Set Intention	Assess Action
Morning Gratitude	☐	☐
The Two-Minute Rule	☐	☐
Curious Moments	☐	☐
Kind Attention	☐	☐
Resilience Thinking	☐	☐

An insight I learned today:_____

_____

Date: _____ / _____ / _____ Day _____

Practices	Set Intention	Assess Action
Morning Gratitude	☐	☐
The Two-Minute Rule	☐	☐
Curious Moments	☐	☐
Kind Attention	☐	☐
Resilience Thinking	☐	☐

An insight I learned today:_____

_____

No need to be embarrassed by your irrational imaginations. They are a norm for everyone. Just don't act on them & reduce their dose.

Date: _____ / _____ / _____ Day _____

Practices	Set Intention	Assess Action
Morning Gratitude	☐	☐
The Two-Minute Rule	☐	☐
Curious Moments	☐	☐
Kind Attention	☐	☐
Resilience Thinking	☐	☐

An insight I learned today:_____

_____

Date: _____ / _____ / _____ Day _____

Practices	Set Intention	Assess Action
Morning Gratitude	☐	☐
The Two-Minute Rule	☐	☐
Curious Moments	☐	☐
Kind Attention	☐	☐
Resilience Thinking	☐	☐

An insight I learned today:_____

_____

Our source of stress and joy are the same. Wishing away all the stressors would be wishing away life.

Date: _____ / _____ / _____ Day _____

Practices	Set Intention	Assess Action
Morning Gratitude	☐	☐
The Two-Minute Rule	☐	☐
Curious Moments	☐	☐
Kind Attention	☐	☐
Resilience Thinking	☐	☐

An insight I learned today:_____

_____

Date: _____ / _____ / _____ Day _____

Practices	Set Intention	Assess Action
Morning Gratitude	☐	☐
The Two-Minute Rule	☐	☐
Curious Moments	☐	☐
Kind Attention	☐	☐
Resilience Thinking	☐	☐

An insight I learned today:_____

_____

Do not multitask in relationships. Partial presence could be worse than absence.

Date: _____ / _____ / _____ Day _____

Practices	Set Intention	Assess Action
Morning Gratitude	☐	☐
The Two-Minute Rule	☐	☐
Curious Moments	☐	☐
Kind Attention	☐	☐
Resilience Thinking	☐	☐

An insight I learned today:_____

_____

Date: _____ / _____ / _____ Day _____

Practices	Set Intention	Assess Action
Morning Gratitude	☐	☐
The Two-Minute Rule	☐	☐
Curious Moments	☐	☐
Kind Attention	☐	☐
Resilience Thinking	☐	☐

An insight I learned today:_____

A negative event assigned a positive meaning feels less negative.
However, the deeper the hurt, the longer it takes to find meaning.

Date: _____ / _____ / _____ Day _____

Practices	Set Intention	Assess Action
Morning Gratitude	☐	☐
The Two-Minute Rule	☐	☐
Curious Moments	☐	☐
Kind Attention	☐	☐
Resilience Thinking	☐	☐

An insight I learned today:_____

_____

Date: _____ / _____ / _____ Day _____

Practices	Set Intention	Assess Action
Morning Gratitude	☐	☐
The Two-Minute Rule	☐	☐
Curious Moments	☐	☐
Kind Attention	☐	☐
Resilience Thinking	☐	☐

An insight I learned today:_____

Relationships are one of the most important aspects of work. Jobs enhancing relationships improve wellbeing & even longevity.

Date: _____ / _____ / _____ Day _____

Practices	Set Intention	Assess Action
Morning Gratitude	☐	☐
The Two-Minute Rule	☐	☐
Curious Moments	☐	☐
Kind Attention	☐	☐
Resilience Thinking	☐	☐

An insight I learned today:_____

_____

Date: _____ / _____ / _____ Day _____

Practices	Set Intention	Assess Action
Morning Gratitude	☐	☐
The Two-Minute Rule	☐	☐
Curious Moments	☐	☐
Kind Attention	☐	☐
Resilience Thinking	☐	☐

An insight I learned today:_____

_____

No work is too small or large. As long as you serve with passion and joy, your work can provide you a deeper meaning.

Creative Immersion #13

What is forgiveness?

_____

_____

What are the benefits of forgiveness?

_____

_____

_____

Do you have someone you wish to forgive?

_____

_____

What might be the next best steps for you to begin your forgiveness journey?

_____

_____

_____

Suggested activities for the next two weeks:
- ◊ Think about the meaning of the word spirituality for you.
- ◊ What is the connection between spirituality, meaning, and forgiveness?

Date: _____ / _____ / _____ Day _____

Practices	Set Intention	Assess Action
Morning Gratitude	☐	☐
The Two-Minute Rule	☐	☐
Curious Moments	☐	☐
Kind Attention	☐	☐
Resilience Thinking	☐	☐

An insight I learned today:_____

_____

Date: _____ / _____ / _____ Day _____

Practices	Set Intention	Assess Action
Morning Gratitude	☐	☐
The Two-Minute Rule	☐	☐
Curious Moments	☐	☐
Kind Attention	☐	☐
Resilience Thinking	☐	☐

An insight I learned today:_____

The quality of your attention has greater effect on the quality of your experience than the details of your task.

Date: _____ / _____ / _____ Day _____

Practices	Set Intention	Assess Action
Morning Gratitude	☐	☐
The Two-Minute Rule	☐	☐
Curious Moments	☐	☐
Kind Attention	☐	☐
Resilience Thinking	☐	☐

An insight I learned today:_____

_____

Date: _____ / _____ / _____ Day _____

Practices	Set Intention	Assess Action
Morning Gratitude	☐	☐
The Two-Minute Rule	☐	☐
Curious Moments	☐	☐
Kind Attention	☐	☐
Resilience Thinking	☐	☐

An insight I learned today:_____

_____

Research shows the opposite of being patient isn't being impatient. It is getting anxious, angry, injured, unwell, even dead.

Date: _____ / _____ / _____ Day _____

Practices	Set Intention	Assess Action
Morning Gratitude	☐	☐
The Two-Minute Rule	☐	☐
Curious Moments	☐	☐
Kind Attention	☐	☐
Resilience Thinking	☐	☐

An insight I learned today:_____

_____

Date: _____ / _____ / _____ Day _____

Practices	Set Intention	Assess Action
Morning Gratitude	☐	☐
The Two-Minute Rule	☐	☐
Curious Moments	☐	☐
Kind Attention	☐	☐
Resilience Thinking	☐	☐

An insight I learned today:_____

_____

> Humility is having accurate self-awareness with low self-focus. Be extra humble toward those who struggle with self-worth.

Date: _____ / _____ / _____ Day _____

Practices	Set Intention	Assess Action
Morning Gratitude	☐	☐
The Two-Minute Rule	☐	☐
Curious Moments	☐	☐
Kind Attention	☐	☐
Resilience Thinking	☐	☐

An insight I learned today:_____

_____

Date: _____ / _____ / _____ Day _____

Practices	Set Intention	Assess Action
Morning Gratitude	☐	☐
The Two-Minute Rule	☐	☐
Curious Moments	☐	☐
Kind Attention	☐	☐
Resilience Thinking	☐	☐

An insight I learned today:_____

_____

The fear of vulnerability weakens us worse than the vulnerability itself.
You'll become strong when you aren't afraid to be vulnerable.

Date: _____ / _____ / _____ Day _____

Practices	Set Intention	Assess Action
Morning Gratitude	☐	☐
The Two-Minute Rule	☐	☐
Curious Moments	☐	☐
Kind Attention	☐	☐
Resilience Thinking	☐	☐

An insight I learned today:_____

_____

Date: _____ / _____ / _____ Day _____

Practices	Set Intention	Assess Action
Morning Gratitude	☐	☐
The Two-Minute Rule	☐	☐
Curious Moments	☐	☐
Kind Attention	☐	☐
Resilience Thinking	☐	☐

An insight I learned today:_____

_____

Even if you are surrounded by the kindest and most well-meaning people, you'll get hurt. Forgiveness is essential to daily happiness.

Date: _____ / _____ / _____ Day _____

Practices	Set Intention	Assess Action
Morning Gratitude	☐	☐
The Two-Minute Rule	☐	☐
Curious Moments	☐	☐
Kind Attention	☐	☐
Resilience Thinking	☐	☐

An insight I learned today:_____

_____

Date: _____ / _____ / _____ Day _____

Practices	Set Intention	Assess Action
Morning Gratitude	☐	☐
The Two-Minute Rule	☐	☐
Curious Moments	☐	☐
Kind Attention	☐	☐
Resilience Thinking	☐	☐

An insight I learned today:_____

_____

Depending on the context, our weakness can become our strength, and our strength can become our weakness.

Date: _____ / _____ / _____ Day _____

Practices	Set Intention	Assess Action
Morning Gratitude	☐	☐
The Two-Minute Rule	☐	☐
Curious Moments	☐	☐
Kind Attention	☐	☐
Resilience Thinking	☐	☐

An insight I learned today:_____

_____

Date: _____ / _____ / _____ Day _____

Practices	Set Intention	Assess Action
Morning Gratitude	☐	☐
The Two-Minute Rule	☐	☐
Curious Moments	☐	☐
Kind Attention	☐	☐
Resilience Thinking	☐	☐

An insight I learned today:_____

_____

> We aren't physical beings having a physical experience. We are spiritual beings having a spiritual experience.

Creative Immersion #14

What is the meaning of the word spirituality for you?

_____

_____

How is your definition of spirituality connected to meaning and forgiveness?

_____

_____

_____

How is your definition of spirituality connected to being kind to nature?

_____

_____

_____

Anything you can personally do to improve our environment?

_____

_____

_____

Any additional thoughts?

_____

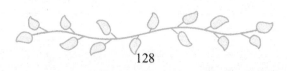

Additional Resources

Books: Mayo Clinic Guide to Stress Free Living
              Mayo Clinic Handbook for Happiness
              Immerse: A 52-Week Course in Resilient Living
              Mindfulness Redesigned for the Twenty-First Century
              Stronger: The Science and Art of Stress Resilience
              SMART: Stress Management and Resilience Training

Websites: Resilientoption.com
              Resiliencetrainer.com
              Myhappinesspal.com

Social Media: @amitsoodmd

Train-the-trainer course: Transform

Please access this link for additional information:
https://www.resiliencetrainer.com/our-solutions-1/

Made in the USA
Las Vegas, NV
26 March 2024

87740385R00075

Alchemy and how the framework supports your endeavors. I would also love to hear your stories of tribal alchemy and how they changed the world. It is truly inspiring when we see and hear about tribes that made alchemy and observe the difference it made. The alchemy of others gives us insight and hope to keep making it in our own world and to believe that doing so matters. To that end, I want to invite you to join the conversation and the learning at www.maketribalalchemy.com. This site is a way to connect with other tribal alchemists, learn more about the concepts, and share your stories. I look forward to learning from you and continuing to explore how we might ingeniously take what we have and turn it into what we need. The world awaits your tribal alchemy.

CONCLUSION

As a writer, there's this interesting moment near the end of a project when you realize all the missing ideas you could have or should have added to the work. For me at least, this realization conjures up two simultaneous feelings: excitement and dread. It's exciting because the concepts contained in the book are still generating in me new and more refined ideas. This means there is the possibility of more alchemy in the future. On the other hand, it surfaces dread because by the end of a writing project I usually can't fathom adding anything more to a book that has already required so much of me. I was recently discussing a concept about Tribal Alchemy with a friend. Toward the end of the conversation she added, "You really ought to add this to the book." My first thought was to run out of the building screaming, "Don't make me do it, please don't make me do it."

Alas, I suppose what I'm saying is that I recognize the incompleteness of this work. I have only scratched the surface of these important ideas. I also realize the incompleteness of myself. I know that my ideas evolve and grow as I evolve and grow. I also know that I evolve and grow through the insights and challenges of others.

My sincere hope is that this book generates a rich and meaningful conversation about the process and practices of Tribal Alchemy. I would love to be in many of those conversations, learning how you create Tribal